FM Fine Art Gallery
Los Angeles, CA

September 2016

My Own Private Moon

Curated by Karrie Ross

My Own Private Moon

Curated by Karrie Ross

Karrie Ross: 708 W. 140th Street, Gardena, CA 90347
Visit her website at www.KarrieRoss.com.

My Own Private Moon

Exploring a relationship with five of the Moon's phases.

My Own Private Moon explores the personal relationship of the artists to the moon, their connection to it, interpretation of and with this magical iconic wonder that is so distant and yet very much part of our world. Its gravitational push and pull manipulating emotional well-being, individually and collectively, and movements of oceans high and low tides are an ever present part of our physical and emotional environment. Songs, photos, movies, paintings, all address its wonder. Its images show up in folklore and varying beliefs. We attribute a face to the Moon, a consciousness, a being inside that controls—no wonder the Moon's phases have historically been linked with the word "lunatic." Astrologically, the Moon represents the inner nature of a person and its sign reveals a person's emotional and subconscious state.

A few interesting facts about the Moon:

- The Earth and the Moon revolve together, from Earth, we always see the same side of the Moon!
- There is no "dark side" of the Moon. All parts of the Moon see sunlight equally.
- Not all full Moons are the same size.
- The Moon is not round!
- In 1665 Earths' moon became known as Moon.

The inspiration for the exhibition title came from the movie "My Own Private Idaho" where two best friends…embark on a journey of self discovery and find their relationship stumbling along the way."

A journey of surprise and wonder…acceptance of self, others, and differences of human nature.

My Own Private Moon

21 Los Angeles based Artists

Dave Lovejoy

Roxene Rockwell

Ted Meyer

Wini Brewer

Susan Lizotte

Stevie Love

Bibi Davidson

Cathy Weiss

Sharon Suhovy

Barbara Nathanson

Scott Dienhart

Bryan Ida

Denis Richardson

Ron Therrio

Peggy Sivert

Ada Pullini Brown

Jill Sykes

Ashley Bravin

Lena Moross

Francisco Alvarado

Karrie Ross

My Own Private Moon

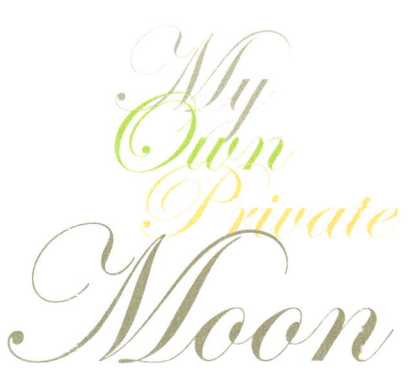

My Own Private Moon

September 2016

My Own Private Moon

Dave Lovejoy
My Own Private Moon

My work often arises from imagining "what if?". I wonder what something would look like, and then I build the thing to find out. For My Own Private Moon, I imagined that the dark side of the moon lies in the shadow of a billboard-like structure; that the dark we see from Earth is a ruse, creating and hiding actual dark. I also like how the structures create their own manipulation of light and shadow under gallery lighting.

The moon and I are old friends, he's lit my path on many hikes and late nights in the studio.

www.lovejoyart.com

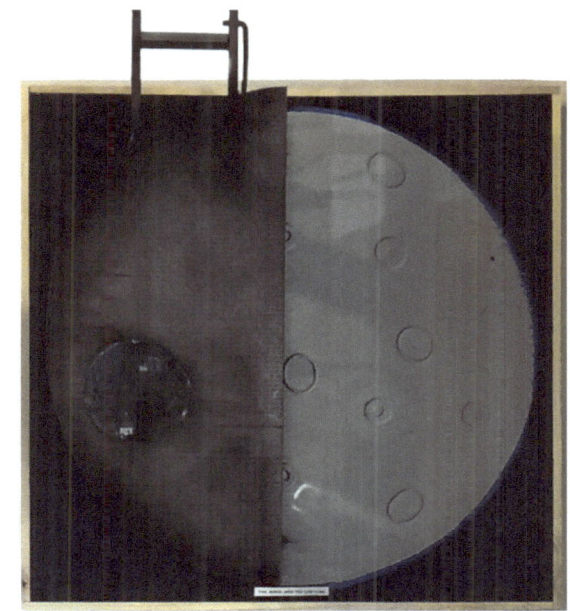

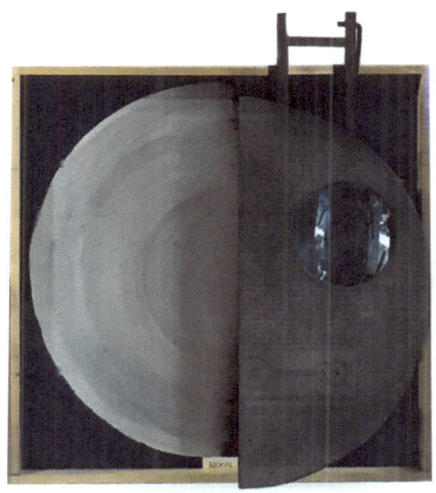

The Moon and Its Craters
mixed media
16" x 16" x 5"

Drawn and Quartered
mixed media
12" x 12" x 4.5"

September 2016

Roxene Rockwell

My Own Private Moon

Moonlight

At dawn, just before the sun rises,
when the moon lights the earth,
I rise and go running.
My head is uncovered.
My face barren
of sunscreen.

My path is lit not by the sun,
or streetlights,
but from the moon.

As my feet hit the ground
I tilt my face upward to capture the light
   rays from the moon.
Such a peaceful time of day
to get my daily dose of sunlight.

www.roxenerockwell.com

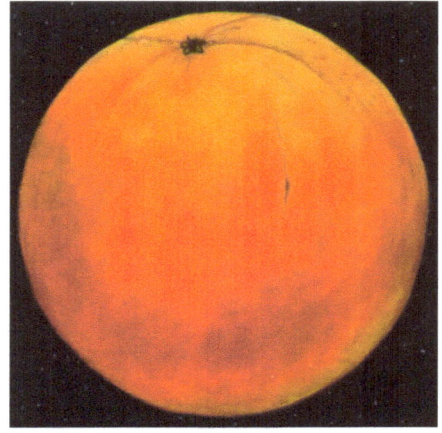

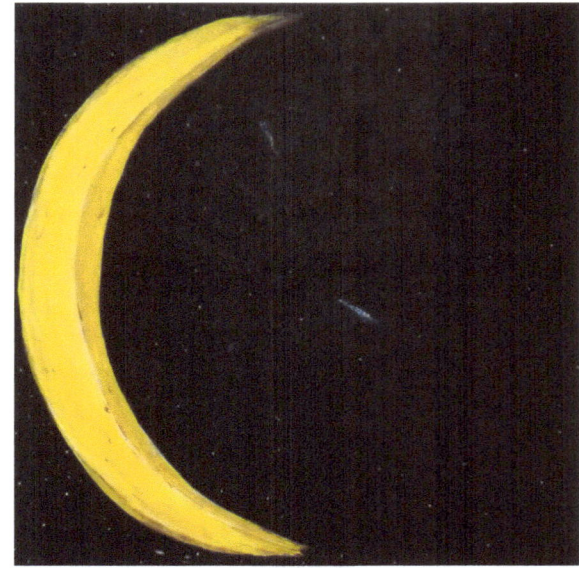

Full Moon c. 2016
Collage and acrylic paint
   on a wood panel
8" x 8"

Crescent Moon c. 2016
Collage and acrylic paint
   on a wood panel.
12" x 12"

Ted Meyer

My Own Private Moon

I travel a lot and when I miss people back home I always think about the Moon and how it links us together.

When the people I care about back home look up at the night sky they are seeing the same moon I see on my travels.

www.tedmeyer.com

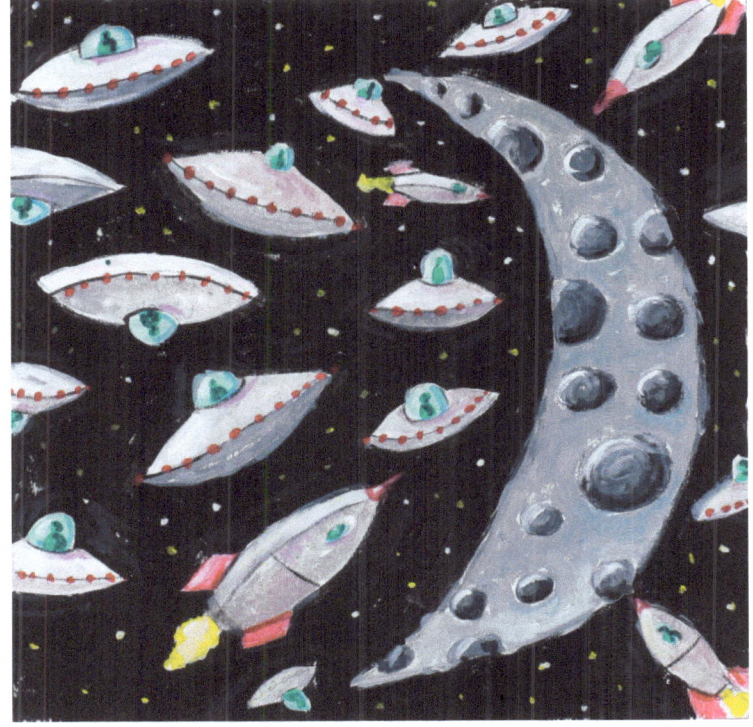

Rush Hour
Acrylic on Panel
12" x 12"

Wini Brewer
My Own Private Moon

The Moon and Me

Mother Goose taught me about the night.
Her moon is my moon, a Mother Goose moon.

I grew up under inky black bedtime skies, looking
up each night in childhood wonder.

"Twinkle, twinkle, little star,
How I wonder what you are."

Biggest of all was the moon. My books were filled
with tales of old man moon. I searched for the man
in the moon my Dad said resided there.

There were visions of cows jumping over the moon
or travelers sailing off in a wooden shoe.

"Where are you going, and what do you wish?"
The old moon asked Wynken, Blynken, and Nod

In my young adulthood, I was almost disappointed
when the first humans landed on the moon. The
old moon would have laughed and sang a song.

www.winibrewer.com

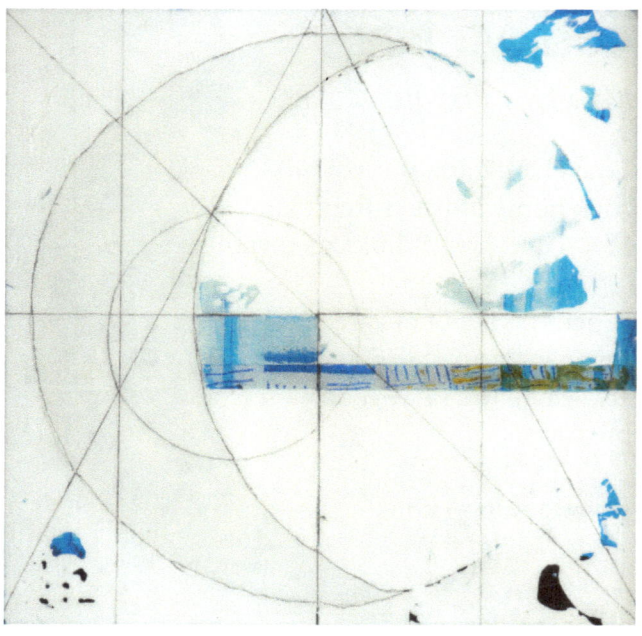

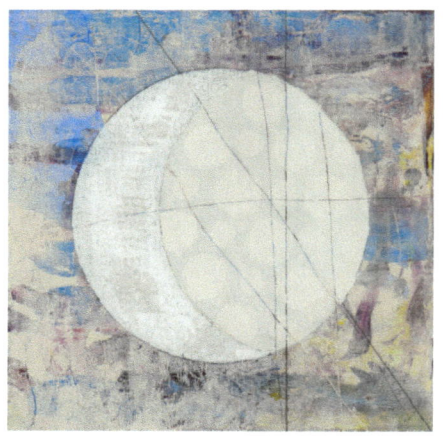

Crescent Moon 1
Acrylic on canvas
12" x 12"

Crescent Moon 2
Acrylic on canvas
9.5" x 9.5"

Susan Lizotte

My Own Private Moon

My thoughts on my Moon:
To look up at night
To be outside
Basking in soft moonlight
Makes me feel connected
To all
Who have lived
Before me
And after I am gone
My Moon makes me feel
Anything is possible
My Moon is the magic
Of being alive

http://www.susanlizotte.com

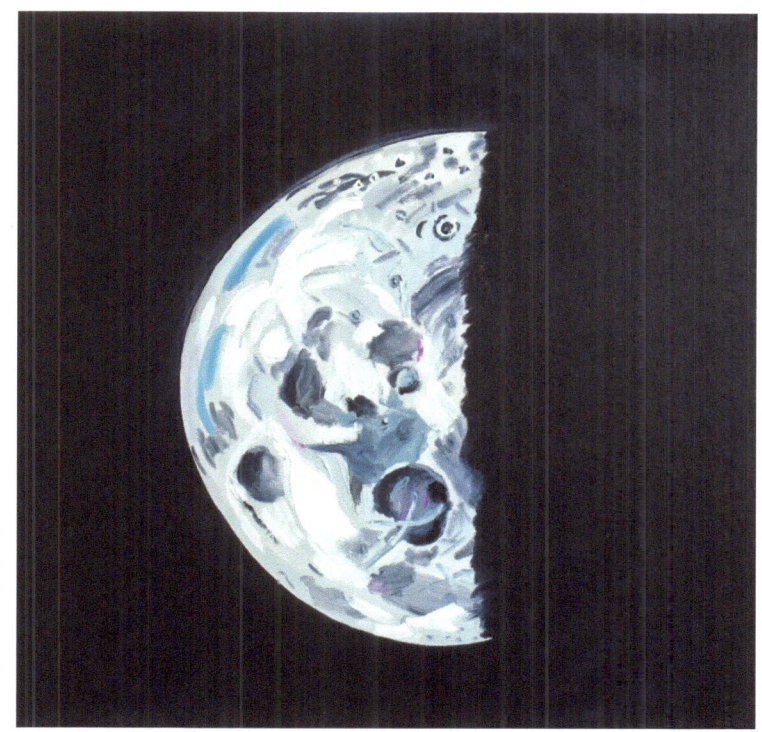

Half Moon
oil on canvas
20" X 20"

September 2016

Stevie Love

My Own Private Moon

The moon has magic in it. We can see that it's an orb hanging suspended moving through space and by extrapolation we know in the depths of our being that our earth is the same. The moon shines on us at night being the yin female energy to the sun's daytime yang male energy. We know the moon has a powerful effect on our planet moving the seas in their rhythm and I feel the metaphor of our connection to the wider universe and the reciprocal effects of all the objects in the universe upon every other object including our own hearts and minds with every living thing (and all things are living). The moon tells us that we are in the universe and the universe is in us.

www.stevielove.com

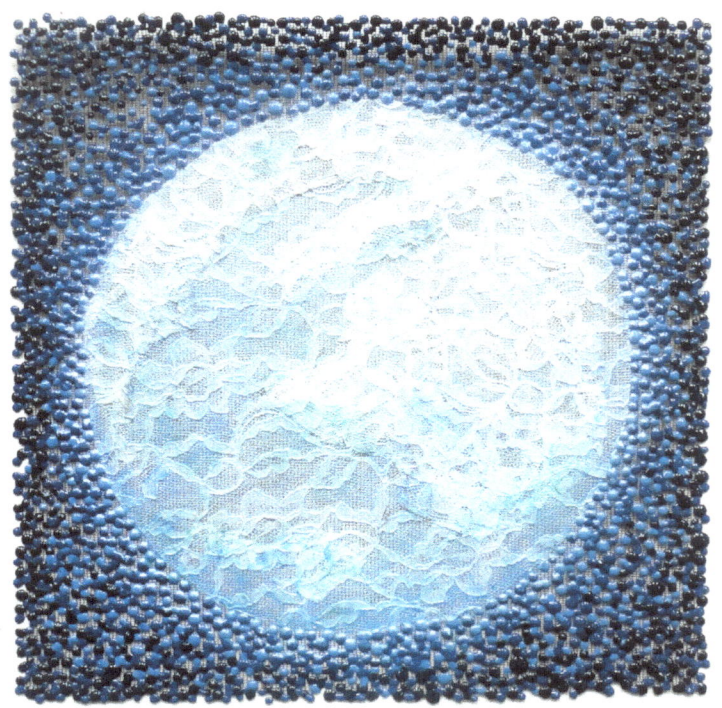

Rabbit Moon
Acrylic paint, lace, poly mesh
16" x 16"

Bibi Davidson

My Own Private Moon

My life holds a forever longing for
a missing piece inside me. The sky is
a vast ocean of unknown memories
and mysteries. When I look up at the
sky, the moon seems to be almost closed
by with a big comforting face, In that
moment, it feels like a friend above
connects me to my childhood fairy
tales and reassuring me about my
own existing.

Once in a blue moon describes the
mystery of the face on the moon seen
from down below.

Once in a red moon shows my accumu-
lated tears pouring out in a storm.

www.bibidavidson.com

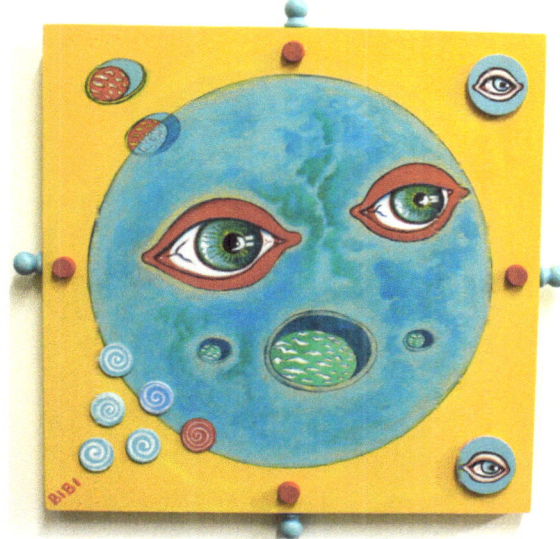

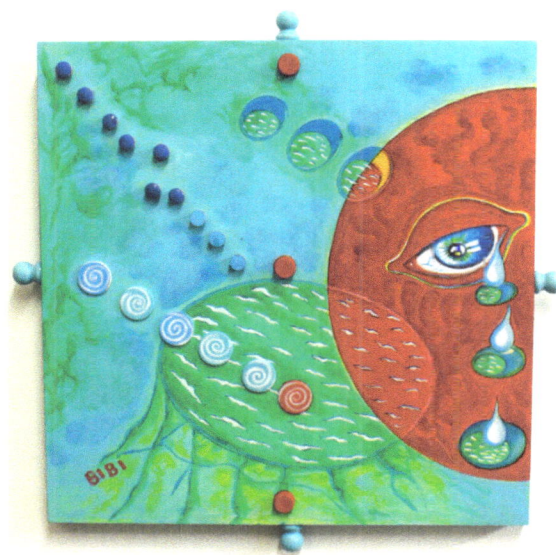

Once In a Blue Moon
acrylic
12" x 12"

Once In a Red Moon
acrylic
12" x 12"

Cathy Weiss
My Own Private Moon

Blue Moon Child

She was born under the full moon of Cancer
Lighting our way out of the darkness,
Intuitive, powerful and creative
She is the interstice of consciousness,
  a soul child
Embracing life watching over
Tides, seasons, plants and animals of the
  night
A goddess of strength and maturity
Blue, the color of protection
She is magical, a blue moon child

www.Cathyweissink.com

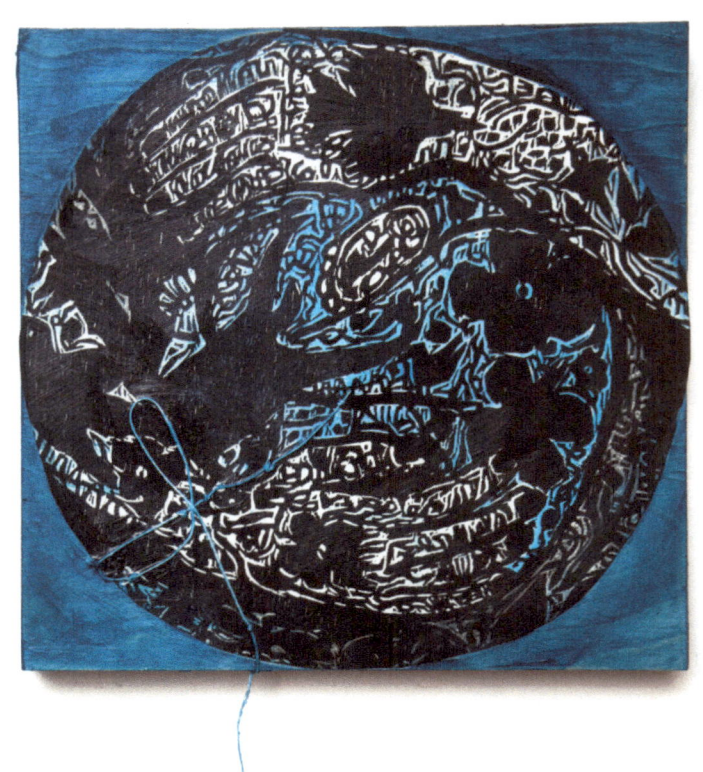

Blue Moon Child
mixed media
12" x 12"

Sharon Suhovy

My Own Private Moon

The moon is the companion of sailors. I'm a sailor. I owned a sailboat for about 4 years. When I sailed at night it seemed like I could reach out and touch the moon. The moonlight would illuminate the sea, and twinkle on the steel gray water. The moon was my mysterious magical orb. It gave me comfort, balance, and orientation. Sailing with a waxing moon was spectacular because the moon would grow brighter each night. The mystery of moonlight though is that everything is colorless, and that the world is a spectacular range of grays.

www.facebook.com/pages/Sharon-Suhovy/157946574216476

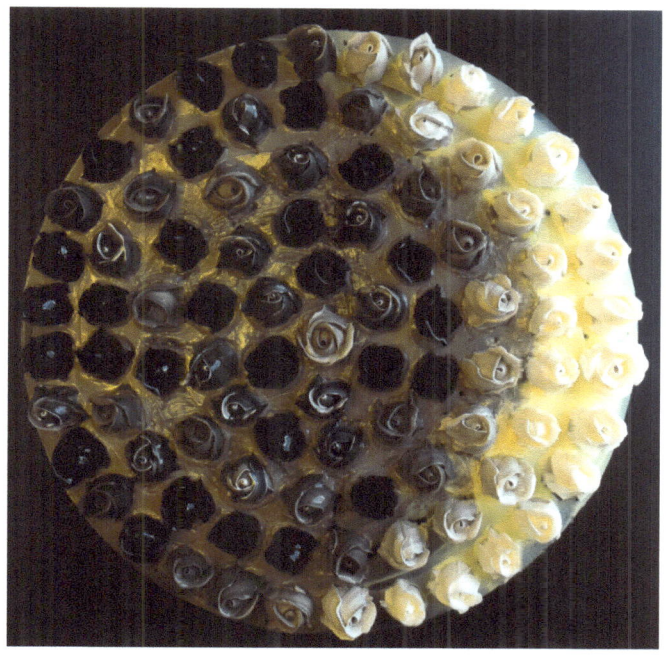

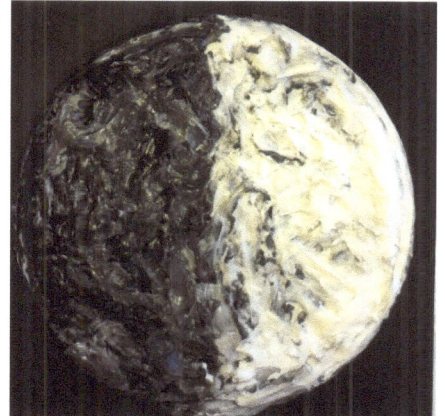

Waxing Crescent Moon' Birth Days.
Acrylic on wood.
24" x 24" x 5"

Waxing Quarter Moon' Sailing.
Acrylic on wood.
12" x 12" x 3"

Barbara Nathanson

My Own Private Moon

Just as the moon reveals and conceals its' face to earthlings – my relationship with the big white globe has spanned my human growth phases. From evenings of young love under a full moon to eventual mature love through various moon phases. Some evenings, while moon gazing, the atmosphere felt charged with electric excitement! A night filled with imaginative possibilities! Ahh, "that old devil moon in my eyes". Just makes one need to put those feelings on a canvas.

www.barbara-nathanson.com

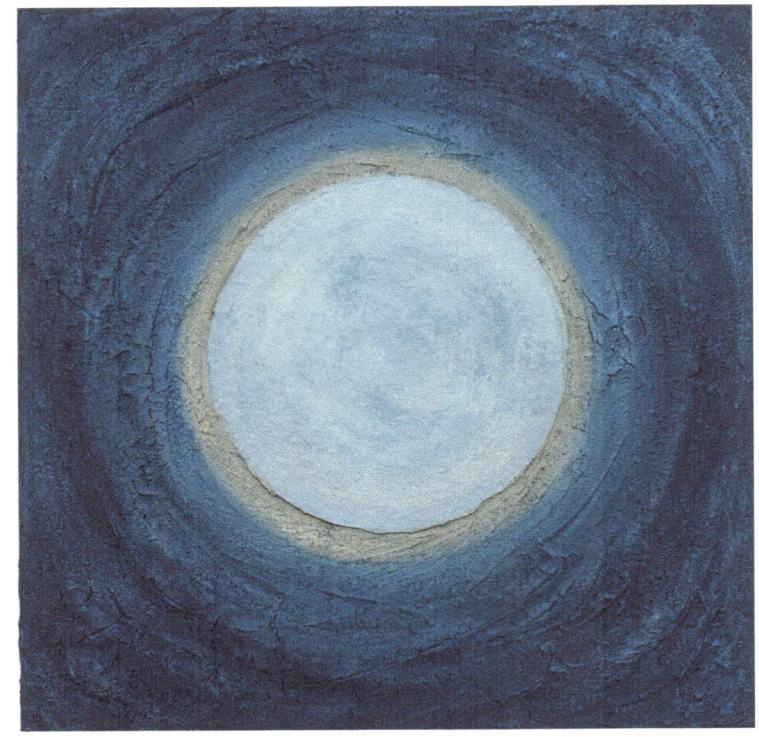

HALO
acrylic on canvas
24" x 24"

Scott Dienhart
My Own Private Moon

I have always had a penchant for fantasy art. When this opportunity surfaced I was eager to get to it. No matter where you are on this Earth the moon is always a constant. It has always been a stepping stone for my imagination. Always inspirational to look toward the moon, connect the dots with other visible planets and step off into worlds beyond our grasp except for those of the imagination. "Lunar Breeze" came to life as a faint vision and morphed itself into what you are looking at today.

www.scottdienhart.com

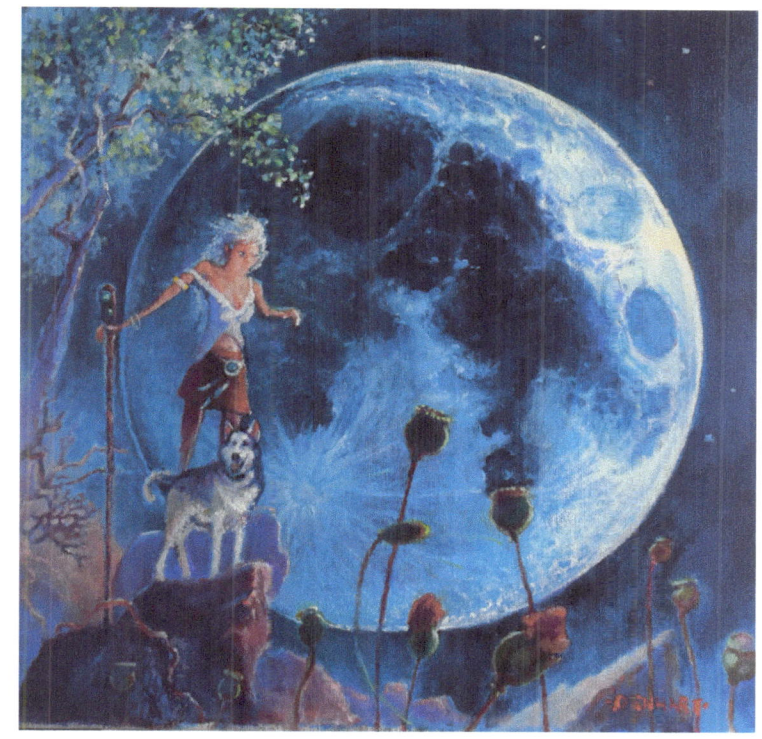

Lunar Breeze
Oil on Canvas
12" x 12"

Bryan Ida
My Own Private Moon

I am an avid fisherman and I observe the phase of the Moon and its timing and how it affects fish behavior.

Tidal movements and light on the water have influence on fishing and by observing and cataloging time of year and moon phase when I fish, I build a reference for future endeavor.

www.bryanida.com

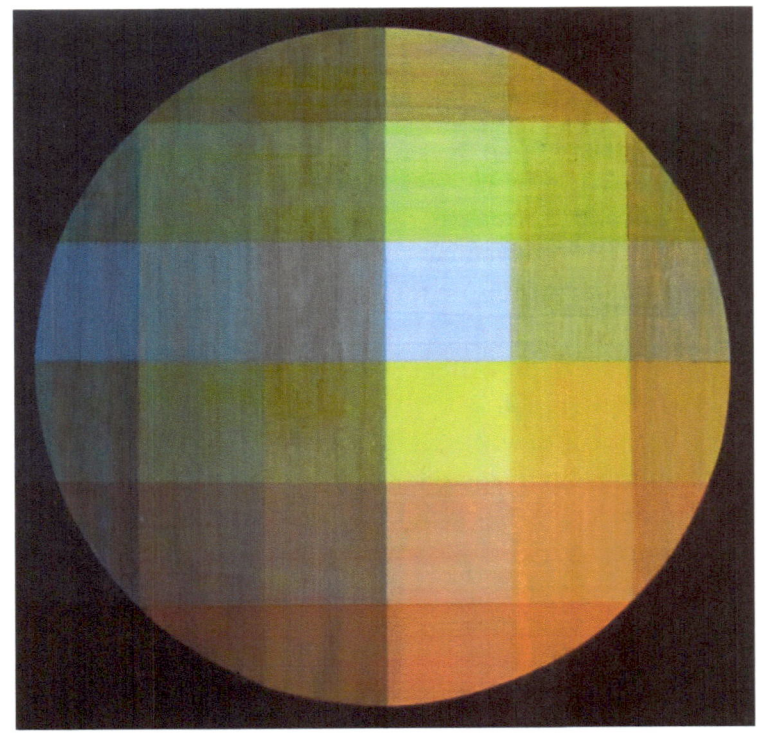

Half Moon
acrylic and ply on panel
12" x 12"

Denis Richardson

My Own Private Moon

Catching an unexpected glimpse of the
moon on most days is like a cosmic
check. The earth's twin reminds me of
my place in the solar system. A signal to
breathe awareness into my actions.
It's a call to action. Sometimes I look
for it, waiting for it to appear in a new
shape or place. In my family the moon
reminds us of our love connections,
however slippery.

www.DenisRichardson.com

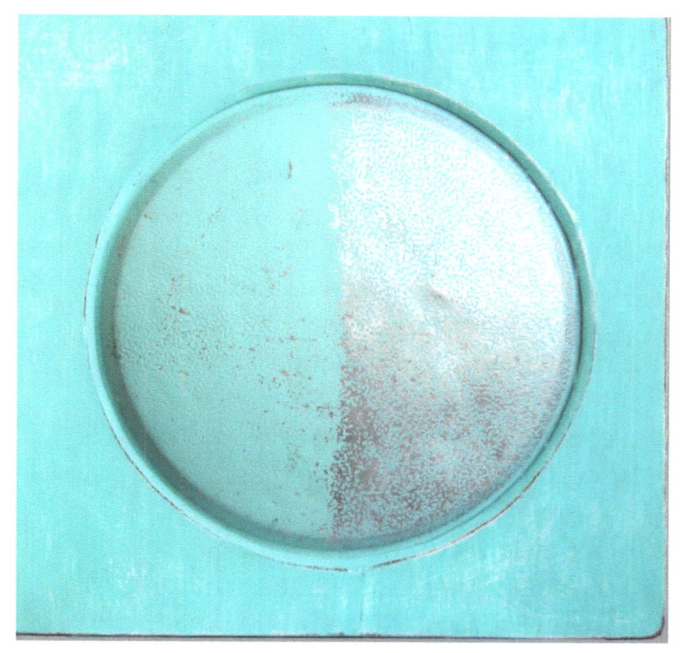

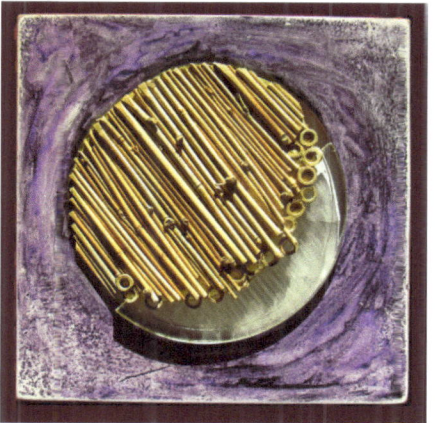

BALANCE
Wood, Metal, Paint
16" x 16"

ECLIPSE
Wood, Glass, Bamboo, Paint
12" x 12"

September 2016

Ron Therrio

My Own Private Moon

As it see it, this yin and the yang thing of the Moon, our Moon. It shows up to bolster our spirit when we are hopeful and optimistic. It too dogs us and mocks us when we are down. It pushes the tides out and drags them back in again like water swirled in a bowl. Even when obscured by sunlight or clouds it is always their. Yet it is leaving us, striking out on its own. It is slowly moving away (at approximately 1" a year). In Los Angeles, the Earth surface is spinning at approximately 850 mph from west to east, so when you drive east at 70 mph you are traveling at 920 mph. Thusly driving west you are doing a paltry 780 mph! So I ask myself; would it not be more efficient to travel westward in the afternoon/evening of a new moon, when both the sun and the moon are setting to the west thereby taking advantage of the ever so slight gravitational forces they are both exerting? Oh… never mind.

www.rontherrio.com

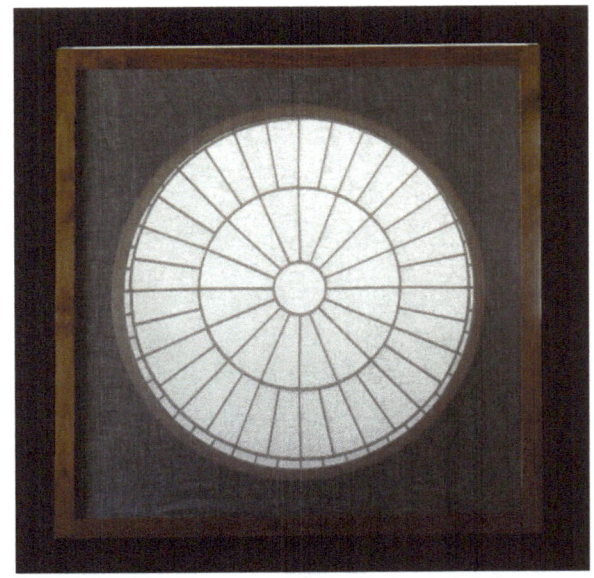

Observitorium
wood, rice paper, cotton
24" x 24"

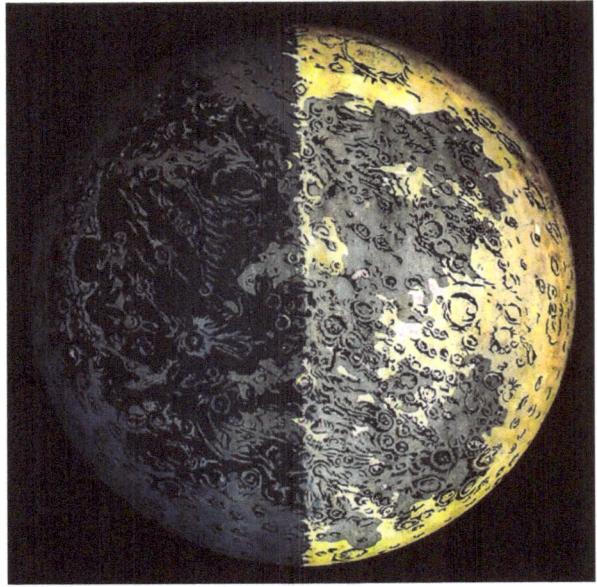

Alabaster Moon (half moon)
plaster, Hemp & black pigment
24" x 24"

Peggy Sivert
My Own Private Moon

The Moon. It shows itself at night – with the light of the sun, its complement. Its very essence is mysterious and magical in the darkness. I love to observe the moon and contemplate its effects on earth. I chose to work with clay to make the 5 phases of the moon in order to show my idea of its beauty and organic nature.

www.peggysivert.com

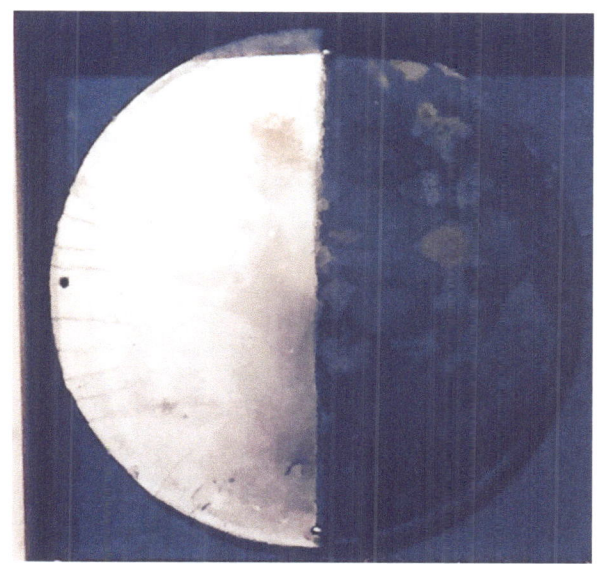

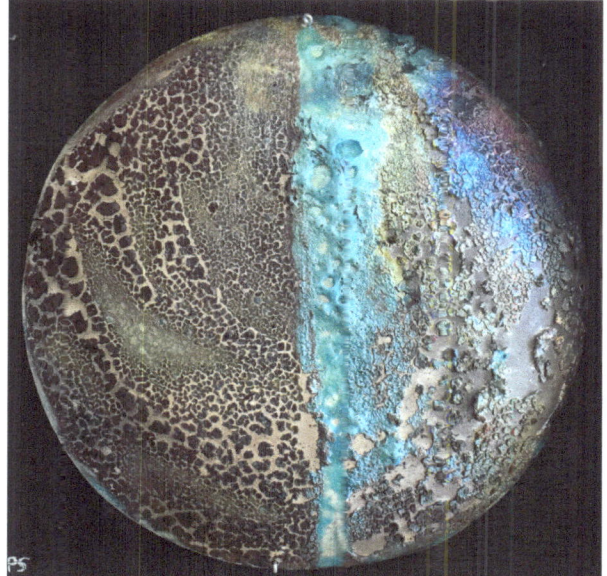

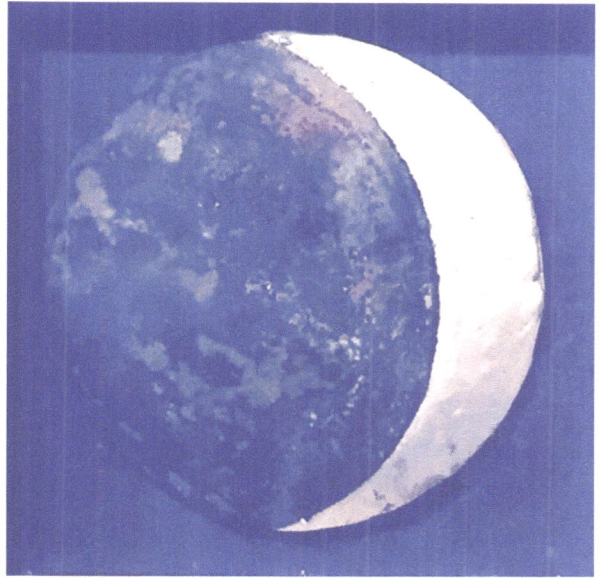

Wild Half
Ceramic Raku fired
8"x 8" x 3"

"1/2"
Ceramic, Raku fired
8"x8" x 3"

Crescent
Ceramic, Raku fired
8"x 8" x 3"

Ada Pullini Brown

My Own Private Moon

Everyone is asleep
there is nothing to come between
the moon and me
     ~Enomoto Siefu-Jo

First day of Autumn
my heart is pounding wild
Ah! The full moon
     ~Basho

The moon does not revolve around the
earth, they revolve around each other.
The barycenter (common center of
mass) is 4300 km from earth's center.
What a marvelous place to visit — a
dance of gravity more perfect than any
waltz.

No matter where you live on earth,
there is a moon.

(*Please do an internet search on this artist
as there is no website.*)

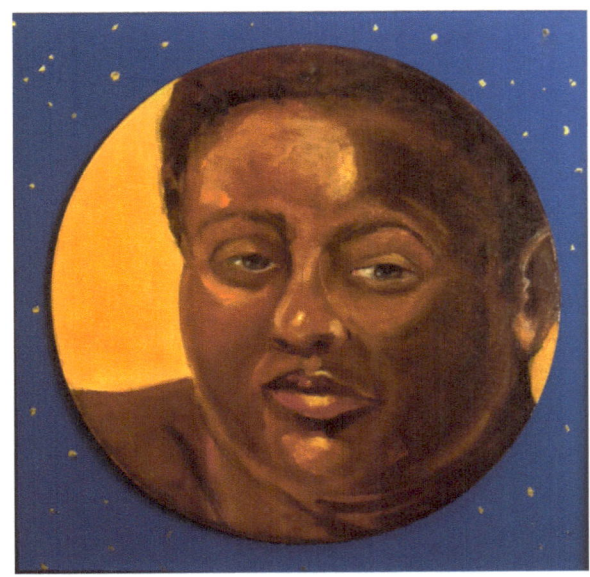

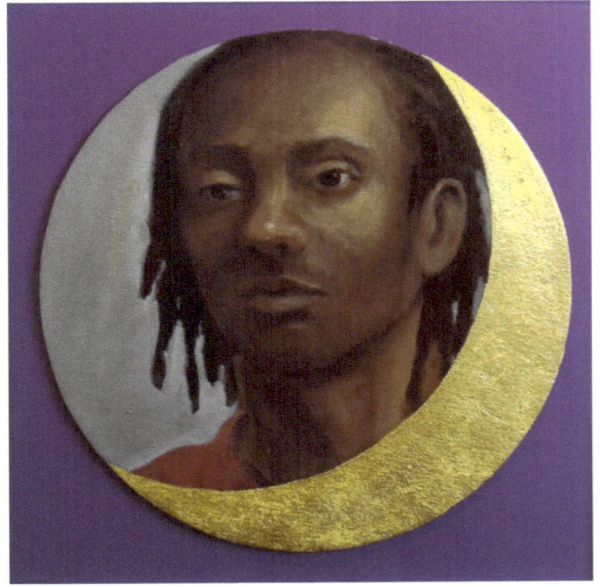

Full Moon Goddess
oil on canvas mounted
on panel
12" x12" framed

Crescent Moon God
oil on canvas, with gold leaf,
mounted on panel
12" x12" framed

Jill Sykes
My Own Private Moon

New Moon
Summer nights gazing out the windows
– I see my mother's laundry hanging on
the line. The bright moonlight over our
yard makes everything glow while we
listen to the crickets.

Mochi Moon
In many Eastern mythologies rather than
the "Man in the Moon" that most of us
grew up with, there is the story of the
"Rabbit in the Moon." He is depicted in
several ways, but most often he is seen
pounding on a mortar and pestle. In
Chinese folklore, the Rabbit is often
portrayed as a companion of the Moon
goddess Chang'e, constantly pounding
the elixir of life for her; but in the Japan-
ese and Korean versions he is pounding
the ingredients for rice cake: a mochi.
There are other similar tales from the
ancient Aztecs as well as many Native
American cultures. My Earth bound
bunny is gazing at his brother in the sky.

www.jillsykes.com

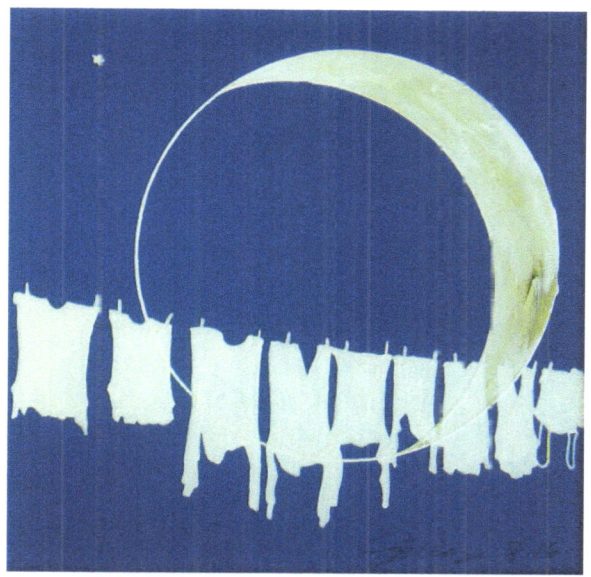

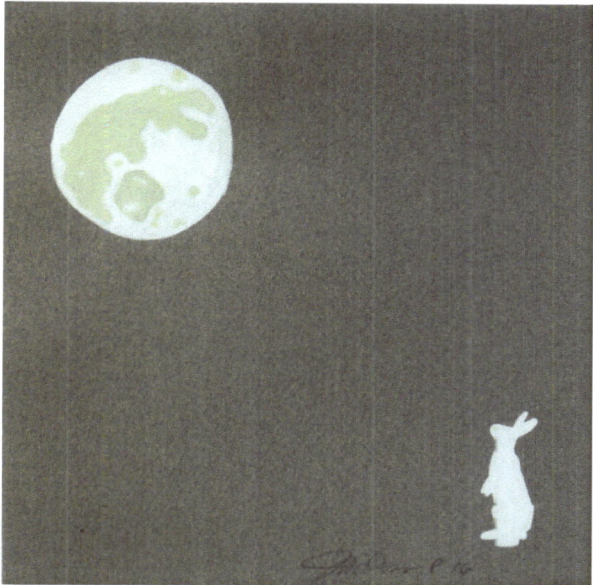

NEW MOON
acrylic on paper
7.5" x 7.5'
   12" x 12" framed

MOCHI MOON
acrylic on paper
7.5" x 7.5"
   12" x 12" framed

Ashley Bravin
My Own Private Moon

My inspiration for "Moon Moths" stems from my time spent as an artist in residence at the Chautauqua Institute in New York. I spent most of those hot summer nights in my lakeside studio, watching the moon wax and wane over the water, guiding all sorts of beautiful nocturnal insects through their nightly rituals. During my time there, I caught several moths, illustrated them, and then ultimately released them back into the moonlight. This is a homage of sorts to those special nights where it was just myself, the moths, and the moon.

http://ashleybravin.com

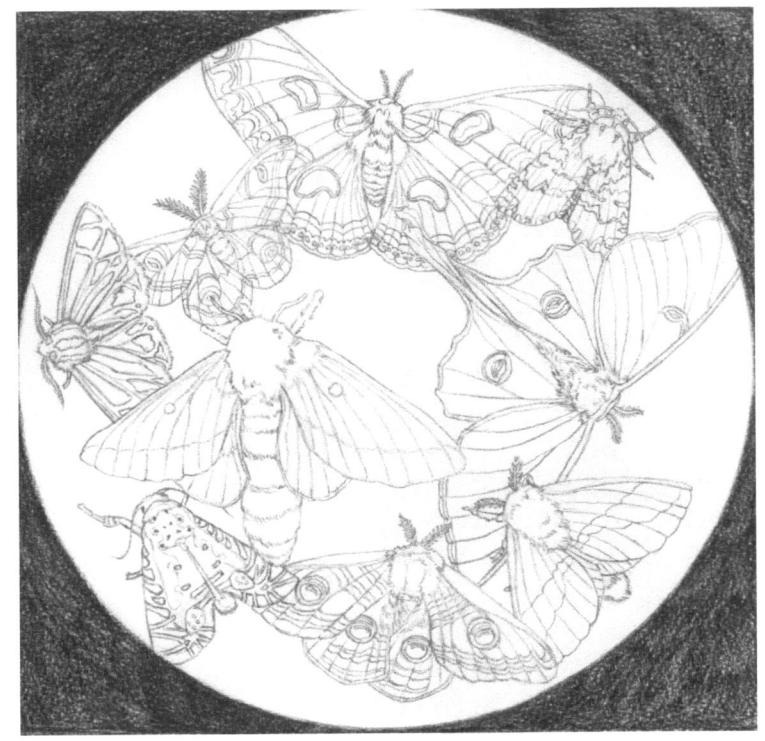

Moon Moths
Graphite on paper
8" x 8"

Francisco Alvarado

My Own Private Moon

My own private moon. Here I go again
being pulled by cosmic forces into
an art show or are the cosmic forces
nudging me into the light?

When I was five or six years old,
growing up in South America one of the
childrenís songs I remember was about
a young bull that is in love with the
reflection of the full moon in a river
where he drinks.

He is happy and playful when the full
moon is there, reflected on the river and
sad when not.

I feel that happy connection and have
created "Moon Vison" for this festive
occasion

http://www.pakoart.com

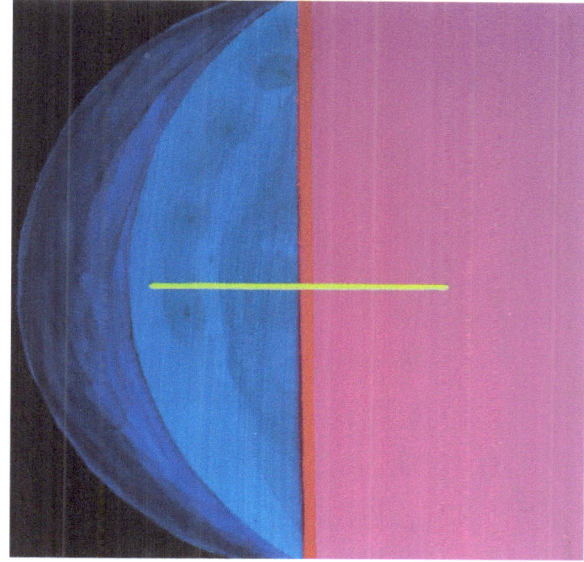

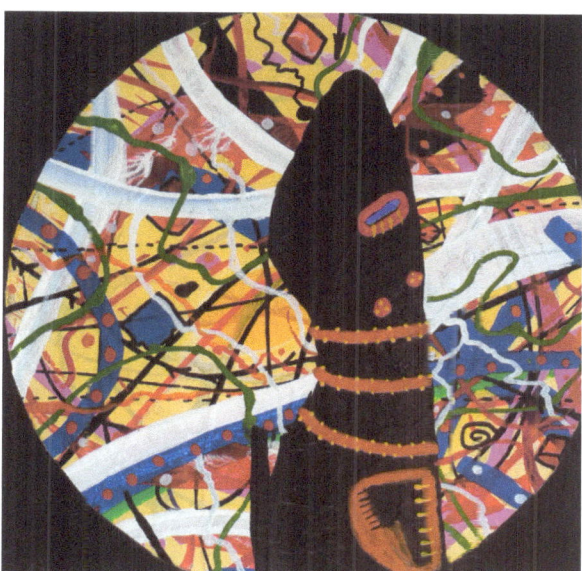

Lazer Focus
acrylic on canvas
10" x 10'

Moon Vision
acrylin on canvas
10" x 10"

September 2016

Lena Moross

My Own Private Moon

Moon. Full moon. Young moon. Half
moon. Half moon?
Half full moon?
Half full glass.
Half empty glass.
That's how my thoughts went about and
around...

www.lenamoross.com

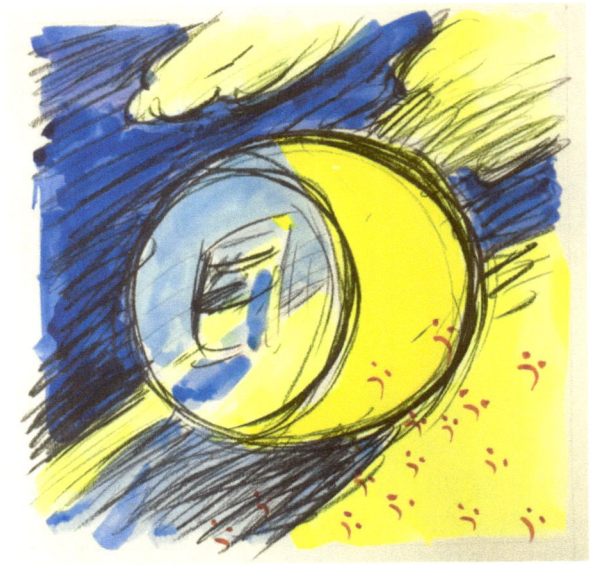

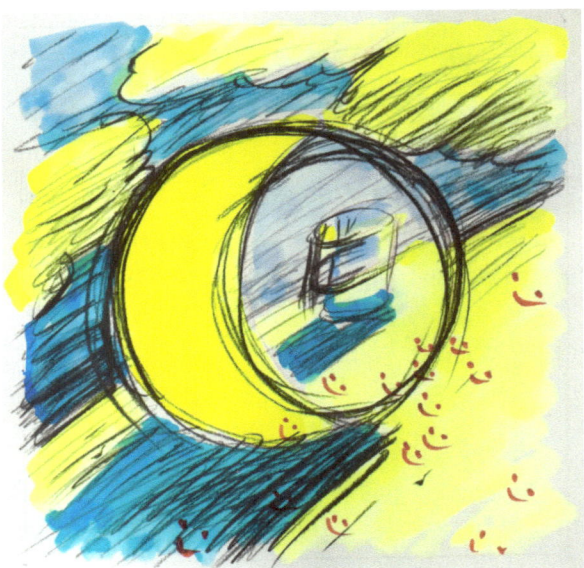

Glass Half Empty
Watercolor, Ink, Paper
16"X16"

Glass Half Full
Watercolor, Ink, Paper
16"X16"

Karrie Ross

My Own Private Moon

*A journey of surprise and wonder…
acceptance of self, others, and differences
of human nature.*

When I was young my family would go
camping in the Angeles Crest Mountains
Each night my Dad would tell us about
the Moon and stars, where was the big
and little dipper, Orions belt, and if the
Moon were full, a story or two. I remember the closeness of family, the light of the
Moon, the shimmer of the stars…and
ways magic of imagination mixed with
the smell of burning wood. I passed these
memories along to my son, the mysteri-
ousness of being able to both see the
Moon even though we were miles apart…
funny and beautiful how something so
obviously simple can mean so much…
I love when he calls to tell me to come
out and look at the Moon.

www.karrieross.com

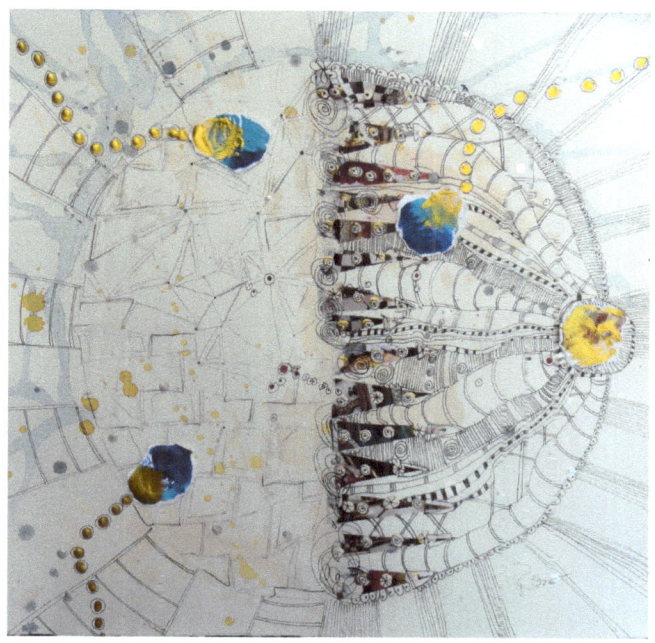

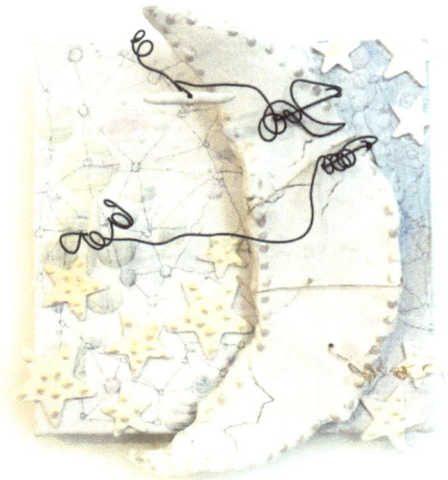

Half Moon Birth
mixed media on paper
12" x 12"

Moon Magic Mapping
mixed media on canvas
8" x 8"

My Own Private Moon

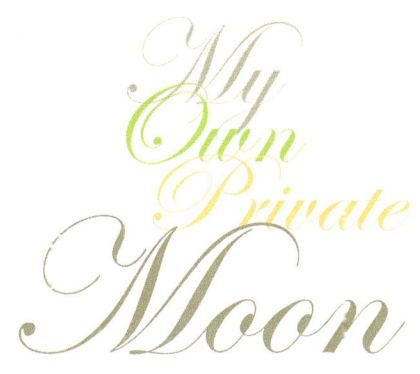

September 2016

My Own Private Moon

My Own Private Moon
Exhibition Photos

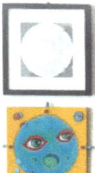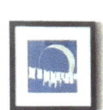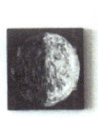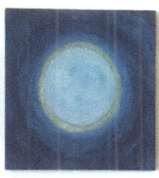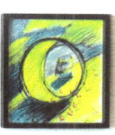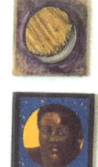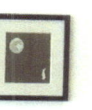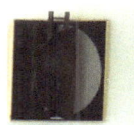

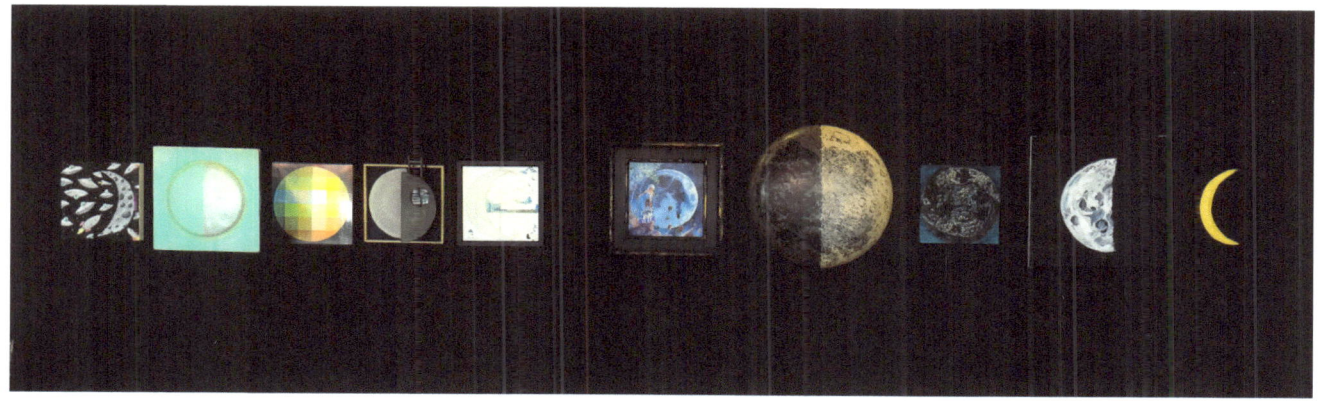

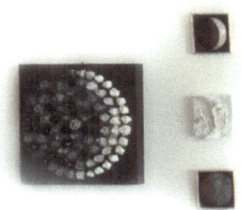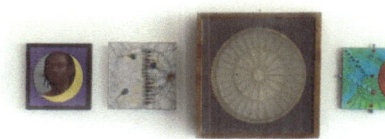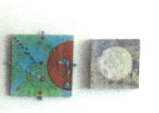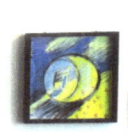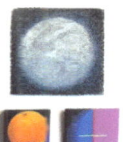

September 2016

My Cwn Private Moon
Exhibition Photos — North Wall

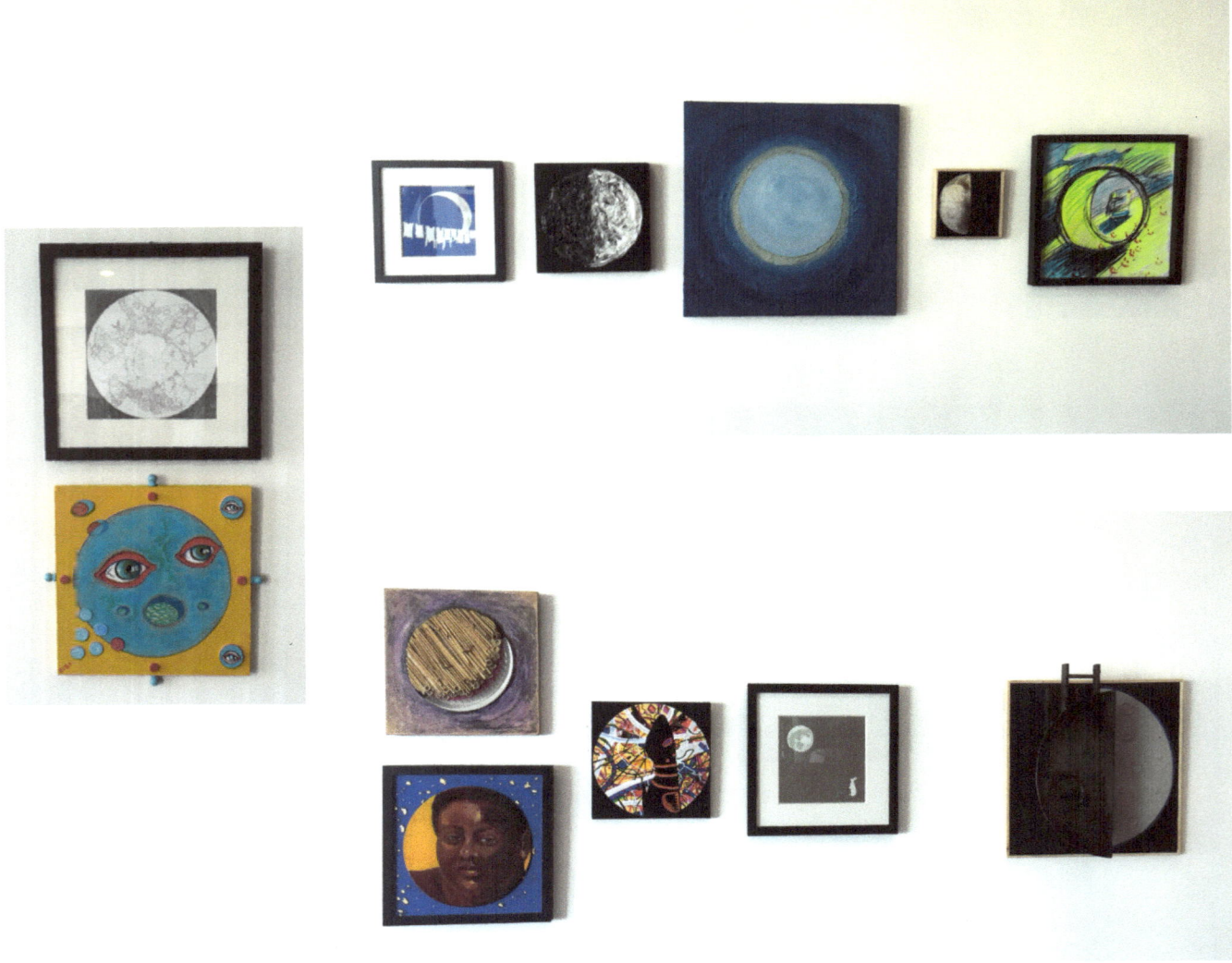

My Own Private Moon
Exhibition Photos — East Wall

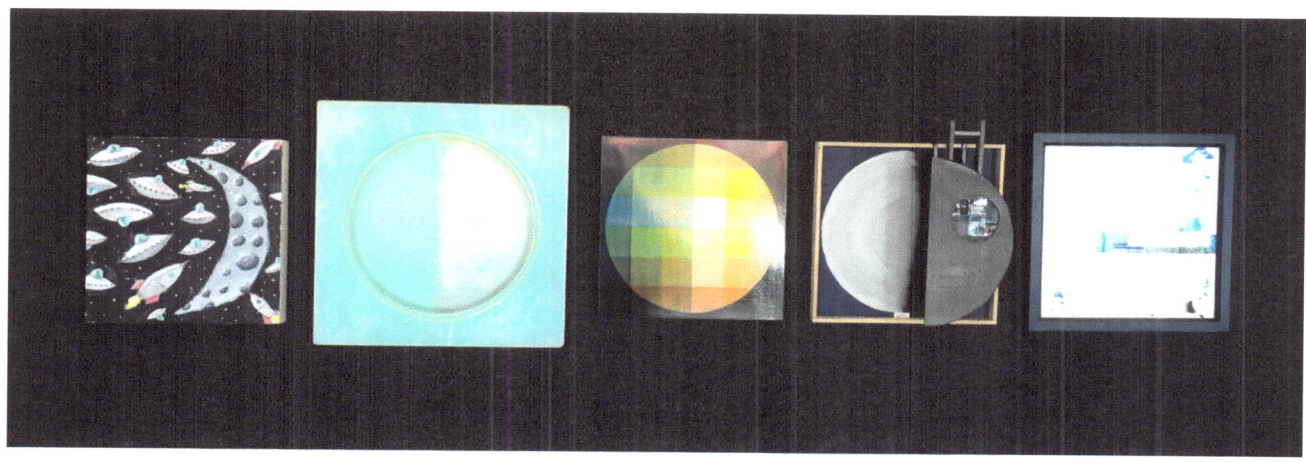

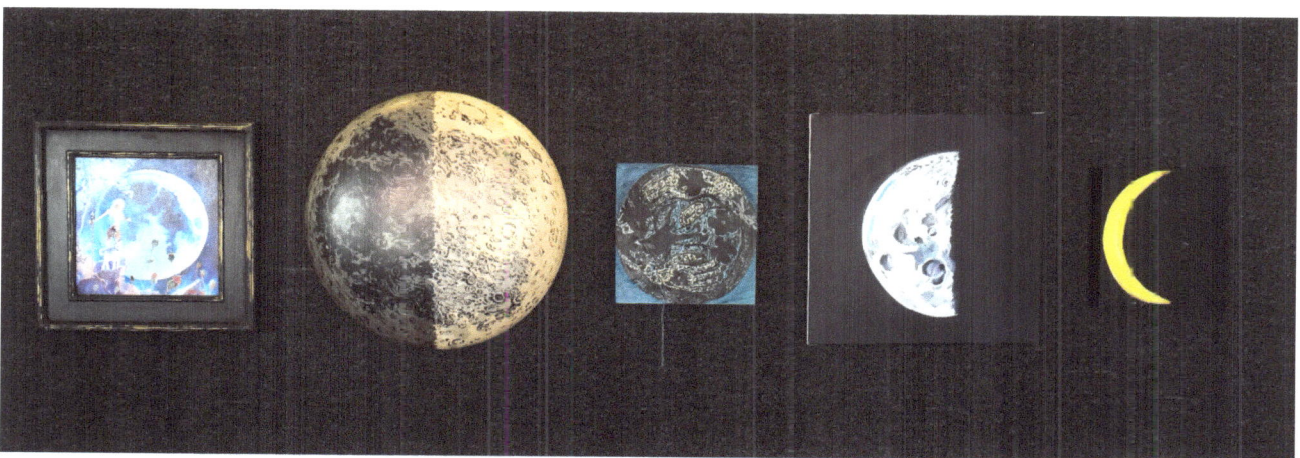

My Own Private Moon
Exhibition Photos — South Wall

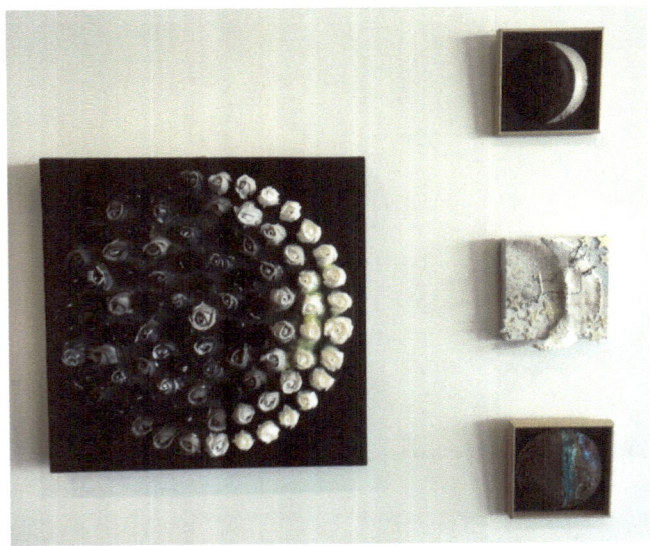
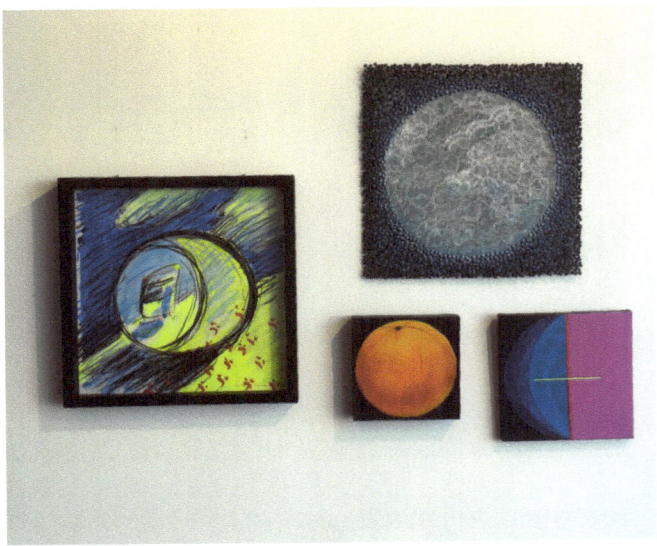
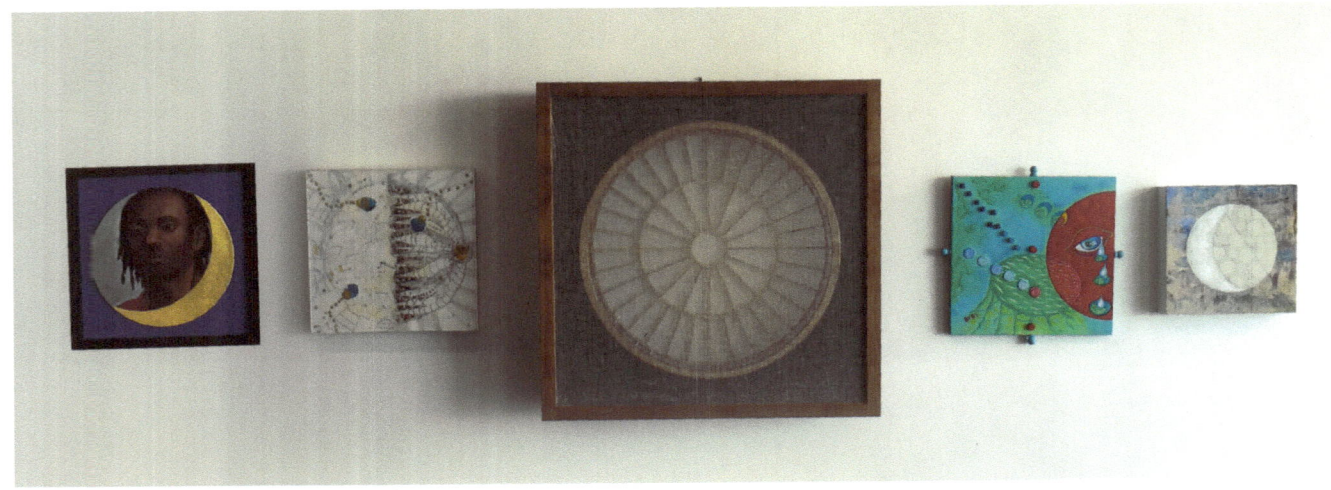

www.ingramcontent.com/pod-product-compliance
Lightning Source LLC
Chambersburg PA
CBHW05090#180526
45159CBC0007B/2815

* 9 7 8 1 5 3 7 4 2 4 4 7 7 *